EXPLORING WORLD CULTURES

Colombia

Alicia Z. Klepeis

Cavendish Square

New York

Published in 2020 by Cavendish Square Publishing, LLC
243 5th Avenue, Suite 136, New York, NY 10016

Website: cavendishsq.com

Library of Congress Cataloging-in-Publication Data

Names: Klepeis, Alicia, 1971- author.
Title: Colombia / Alicia Z. Klepeis.
Description: First edition. | New York : Cavendish Square, [2020] |
Series: Exploring world culture | Includes index. | Audience: Grades 2-5.
Identifiers: LCCN 2018047985 (print) | LCCN 2018049942 (ebook) |
ISBN 9781502647139 (ebook) | ISBN 9781502647122 (library bound) |
ISBN 9781502647108 (pbk.) | ISBN 9781502647115 (6 pack)
Subjects: LCSH: Colombia--Juvenile literature.
Classification: LCC F2258.5 (ebook) | LCC F2258.5 .K55 2020 (print) |
DDC 986.1--dc23
LC record available at https://lccn.loc.gov/2018047985

Editorial Director: David McNamara
Editor: Lauren Miller
Copy Editor: Nathan Heidelberger
Associate Art Director: Alan Sliwinski
Designer: Christina Shults
Production Coordinator: Karol Szymczuk
Photo Research: J8 Media

Printed in the United States of America

Contents

Introduction

Colombia is a country in South America. People have lived here for thousands of years. Different groups have ruled what is now Colombia throughout history. Today, Colombia is a free country. Its government is a **democracy**.

Colombians have many different jobs. Some grow flowers and coffee. Others work in offices, hospitals, hotels, or restaurants. People here also work in factories and mines.

There are many beautiful places to visit in Colombia. There are rain forests, deserts, and ice-capped mountains. There are rivers, swamps, and even some islands. Visitors also come from around the world to enjoy the country's historic cities and beaches.

Music, art, and literature are important parts of Colombian culture. Colombians like eating good food. They also love sports. There are many interesting traditions. Religion is important to many Colombians. Throughout the year, celebrations and festivals take place.

Colombia is an amazing country to explore.

The Cape San Juan beach in northern Colombia's Tayrona National Park is known for its beauty.

Colombia is located in northwestern South America. The Caribbean Sea lies to the north. The Pacific Ocean is west of Colombia. Five countries border Colombia: Brazil, Ecuador, Panama, Peru, and Venezuela.

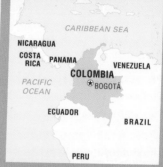

This map shows Colombia and its neighbors.

Colombia covers 439,736 square miles (1,138,910 square kilometers).

The Andes Mountains run through the middle of Colombia. Snow-covered volcanoes can also be

FACT!

Along the coasts and in the eastern plains, Colombia has a **tropical** climate. The nation's highland areas are cooler.

Colombia's Animals and Plants

Colombia is home to lots of different animals and plants. Toucans, sloths, and unique animals like the golden poison frog live here. Plants like mosses, orchids, and cacti grow here too.

Golden poison frogs can usually live for up to ten years.

found here. Colombia's coasts have beaches. There are also desert areas in the north. Huge grasslands, called llanos (YAH-nos), are found in the east.

The Amazon River basin covers almost half of Colombia. This area is in the south. Thick rain forests are here.

The first people in Colombia hunted, gathered seeds and fruits, and fished. Over time, people started farming. They grew crops like corn and potatoes. Groups called the Muisca (or Chibcha) and Sinú lived here.

An illustration of a battle against the Spanish

In 1499, the first Europeans arrived. Spanish explorers wanted to find gold and gems. The Native people tried to protect their

FACT!

In 2016, President Juan Manuel Santos won the Nobel Peace Prize for helping end the civil conflict in Colombia.

Enrique Olaya Herrera

Enrique Olaya Herrera was the president of Colombia from 1930 to 1934. During his presidency, businesses grew and workers gained more rights.

Former Colombian president Enrique Olaya Herrera

land but were defeated. Colombia was under Spanish control until the early 1800s.

After a war against the Spanish in 1819, Colombia became an independent country. Lots of different groups wanted to control the government. This caused civil wars in Colombia that lasted a long time. Many people died. A peace agreement was reached in 2016. Today, Colombians hope for a brighter, peaceful future.

Colombia is a democracy. It has thirty-two departments, like states, and one capital district. The capital of the country is Bogotá.

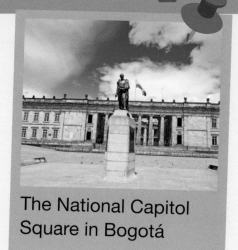

The National Capitol Square in Bogotá

Colombia's government has three parts: legislative, judicial, and executive. The legislative part is called the Congress. Members of the Congress write new laws. Courts make up the judicial part. They follow the country's constitution. The constitution was adopted in

FACT!

All Colombian citizens over the age of eighteen can vote in elections.

Marta Lucía Ramírez

A lawyer and former senator, Marta Lucía Ramírez became the first female vice president of Colombia in August 2018.

Vice President Marta Lucía Ramírez.

1991. It describes all the basic laws of Colombia. Lastly, the executive part includes the president and the **cabinet** ministers. The president runs the government and is the head of state.

Colombia's Congress is made up of two houses, the Senate and the Chamber of Representatives. The Senate has 108 members. The Chamber of Representatives has 171 members. They work in the National Capitol Building.

Colombia has one of Latin America's biggest **economies**. It trades with countries like the United States, China, Panama, and Mexico. The country's money is called the Colombian peso.

A coffee farm near the city of Manizales in western Colombia.

Over 60 percent of Colombian workers have service jobs. Some work in stores, schools, and banks. Others work in restaurants, hospitals,

FACT!

Over 6.5 million tourists from other countries visited Colombia in 2017.

Fabulous Flowers

Colombia is the world's second-largest producer of cut flowers. The country ships over four billion flowers each year to the United States alone!

Roses at the Paloquemao Flower Market in Bogotá.

and offices. The technology industry in Colombia is growing.

Factories in Colombia make lots of things. One everyday example is seats for theaters and sports stadiums. They also produce special things like airplanes and artificial teeth.

Colombian farmers grow crops like coffee, bananas, and sugarcane. Miners drill for petroleum and dig for coal and emeralds in the ground.

The Environment

The Andes Mountains in central Colombia are snowy and rocky. The biggest flying bird in the world, the Andean condor, lives here. Below the mountains, the soil is perfect for growing coffee and other crops.

Some woolly monkeys live for over thirty years.

In the south, the Amazon River basin has beautiful rain forests. Turtles, snakes, and crocodiles live by the river. Anteaters, jaguars, and monkeys live in the thick forests.

FACT!

The Colombian woolly monkey and a bird called the blue-billed curassow are two rare animals from Colombia.

Sadly, forests are being cut down in Colombia for farming and mining. This causes soil **erosion** and destroys the homes of the animals that live there.

A bus adds to air pollution in Bogotá.

Air pollution is also a problem in Colombia. It comes from cars, factories, and burning wood for heating and cooking in the countryside.

Colombia's Clean Energy

Over 70 percent of Colombia's electricity comes from waterpower. The country is also building solar power plants to make energy from the sun.

More than forty-seven million people live in Colombia. Many different **ethnic groups** call Colombia home. Over 84 percent of Colombians are **mestizo** and white.

The second-largest group of people in Colombia have ancestors from Africa and Colombia. They make up about 10 percent of the population. They often live on islands off Colombia's coast, and in the departments of Magdalena and Cauca. Some make a living by

FACT!

The average person in Colombia has a life expectancy of seventy-six years.

The Wayuu People

The Wayuu are Native people who mainly live in the La Guajira desert area. They raise livestock and grow crops.

A Wayuu woman knits a mochila at her home in Uribia, Colombia.

fishing. Just over 3 percent of Colombians have Native Colombian ancestry. That means some of their ancestors were from the first tribes to live in Colombia. Most live in the countryside. Unfortunately, both these groups of people tend to be poorer and have fewer opportunities in Colombia than others.

Most Colombians live in cities and towns. Cities like Bogotá and Medellín are crowded. There, some people live in apartments. Others live in houses. In the city, people can take a bus or ride a bike to work.

This photo shows how big the Ciudad Bolívar area is.

There are also poor, crowded areas like Ciudad Bolívar in Bogotá. These communities are outside the city center. Many people in these areas

FACT!

On average, most Colombian families have two children.

Working Women in Colombia

In the past, most Colombian women did not work outside the home. This is changing. In 2018, 42.9 percent of people working in Colombia were women.

A Bogotá policewoman in uniform.

have a long commute to work each day. Houses here are often small and run-down.

In Colombia's countryside, people commonly work on farms. In mountainous areas, there are coffee farms. In the llanos, ranchers raise cattle and other animals. Mining is also important in some rural areas. For example, gold mining is a big business in the department of Antioquia.

Religion

There is no official religion in Colombia. People are free to believe what they want. However, many people choose to believe in a religion. Most religious people in Colombia are

Tourists visit the Salt Cathedral of Zipaquirá.

Christian. Seventy-nine percent of Colombians are Roman Catholic, and 14 percent are Protestant. Christian Colombians celebrate holidays like Christmas and Easter.

FACT!

The Salt Cathedral of Zipaquirá is a Catholic church located 600 feet (180 meters) underground in an old salt mine.

Native Religions

Colombia's Native peoples often have their own religious beliefs. Followers of these religions usually live in rural areas.

Some people in Colombia follow other religions. In the past, it was considered wrong to practice religions other than Christianity. The right to practice any religion was added to the Colombian constitution in 1991. Today, the nation's Jews tend to live in cities. Colombian Muslims usually live on the nation's Caribbean coast. Some people don't believe in any religion.

The Mosque of Omar ibn al-Khattab in Maicao is the third largest in Latin America.

Language

The most common language in Colombia is Spanish. It is also the only official language in Colombia. The government uses Spanish. Colombians typically use Spanish for business.

Two newspapers, written in Spanish, show Ivan Duque becoming president in 2018.

FACT!

Only three of Colombia's Native languages are spoken by at least fifty thousand people.

Palenquero

Palenquero is a Spanish-based language that was influenced by African languages and Portuguese. Many Palenquero speakers live in the village of San Basilio de Palenque.

Some Colombians speak more than one language. Children in Colombia are taught in Spanish, but schools have English classes too.

Many Native groups have their own languages. There are more than sixty different Native languages spoken in Colombia. Nasa, Emberá, and Wayuu are a few examples. It is believed that about 80 percent of Native people in Colombia can speak their own Native language.

Colombian people create music, art, jewelry, and more. Many Wayuu people make brightly colored woven bags called mochilas. Colombian metalwork is also well known.

Women prepare flowers for the Flower Festival in Medellín.

Tourists from around the world visit Bogotá's Gold Museum to see gold necklaces, masks, and sculptures.

FACT!

Shakira is a Colombian singer who is famous around the world for her Latin music.

The Colombian people celebrate many festivals. At the Flower Festival in Medellín, people create all kinds of artwork using brightly colored flowers.

El Día de las Velitas, or the Day of the Little Candles, is celebrated on December 7. On this day, families light hundreds of small candles along the streets. The candles are meant to guide the spirit of the Virgin Mary as she travels to bless their homes.

Fernando Botero

Fernando Botero is a famous Colombian artist. He is known for his paintings and sculptures. His artwork exaggerates the roundness of both people and animals.

Fun and Play

There are lots of ways to have fun in Colombia. Many Colombians enjoy sports. Soccer is the most popular sport here. People of all ages enjoy playing soccer. Cycling is another well-liked sport.

Sol Abril plays in the 2011 National Tejo Tournament in Bogotá.

Colombia's national sport is *tejo* (TEY-ho). Players throw steel discs (called *tejos*) toward a ring. This ring contains a small parcel filled with gunpowder. If a *tejo* lands on the ring, it will explode!

FACT!

People come from around the world to visit Colombia's fifty-one national parks.

Rock Climbing in Suesca

Located north of Bogotá, Suesca is Colombia's best-known rock climbing spot. It offers adventurous climbers more than four hundred different climbing routes to try!

The rock walls at Suesca are as high as 410 feet (125 meters).

Extreme sports are growing popular in Colombia. Caving, white-water rafting, and bungee jumping are just a few. Along the country's coastline, people also surf and scuba dive.

A traditional kids' game is *trompo*. Players compete by doing tricks with spinning tops. Marbles are also popular with Colombian children.

Food

People in Colombia eat many different foods. Along the coasts and in the Amazon, fish a is common ingredient. Often, it is wrapped in leaves and grilled. Near the Caribbean coast, fish is served with coconut rice.

Papaya, guava, dragonfruit, and pineapple are all found in Colombia.

Sancocho (san-COH-cho) is a delicious soup. It usually contains corn, potatoes, yucca, cilantro,

Coffee is one of the most popular drinks in Colombia.

Desserts in Colombia

Rice pudding is a common dessert in Colombia. So are thin wafers called *obleas* (oh-BLEY-as). They are often served with a caramel-like substance called *arequipe* (ah-rey-KEE-pay) in the middle.

and chicken. People often enjoy it with rice or a slice of avocado.

Arepas (ah-REH-pahs) are a popular bread-like snack made from corn flour. They can be prepared many ways—stuffed with cheese, or even an egg. Tons of fruits are also available in Colombia. Mango, guava, **lulo**, and passion fruit grow here.

29

Glossary

cabinet A group of advisors who help the leader of a country.

democracy A system of government in which leaders are chosen by the people.

economy The use of money and goods in a country.

erosion The wearing away by water, wind, or other natural causes.

ethnic groups Groups of people who share a common culture or ancestry.

lulo A small orange tropical fruit often used in juice.

mestizo A person who has mixed American Indian and European ancestors.

tropical Relating to a climate that is very hot and humid.

Find Out More

Books

Murray, Julie. *Colombia*. Explore the Countries.
Pinehurst, NC: Buddy Books, 2016.

Wiseman, Blaine. *Colombia*. Exploring Countries.
New York: Weigl Publishers, 2016.

Website

Colombia

https://kids.nationalgeographic.com/explore/
countries/colombia/#colombia-dancing.jpg

Video

Exclusive: Rare Ghost Monkeys Filmed in Colombia

https://video.nationalgeographic.com/video/
news/150417-ghost-monkeys-colombia-vin

Index

About the Author

Alicia Z. Klepeis began her career at the National Geographic Society. She is the author of many kids' books, including *Snakes Are Awesome*, *The World's Strangest Foods*, and *A Time for Change*. Klepeis lives with her family in upstate New York.